LITTLE DAISY

and the

SWEARING CLASS

Grace & Truth Books
Sand Springs, Oklahoma

ISBN # 1-58339-0545
First printings, 1800's (dates unknown)
Second printing, Triangle Press, 1990
Third printing, Grace & Truth Books, 2003
Current edition, Grace & Truth Books, 2005

Cover art by Caffy Whitney
Cover design by Ben Gundersen

Grace & Truth Books

3406 Summit Boulevard
Sand Springs, Oklahoma   74063
Phone: 918.245.1500

www.graceandtruthbooks.com

TABLE of CONTENTS

Chapter 1

THE LITTLE FLOWER-GIRL

There stood our Daisy. What a fair, sweet floweret. She looked as pure and sweet as the blossoms over which she bent. She stood beside her basket of flowers. Daisy, with her flowers, was a little spot of brightness and beauty amidst all the dust, heat, and turmoil of the noisy street on that warm summer afternoon.

The street ran beside a large railroad depot. Porters, car-men, and travelers called out, shouting and swearing. Passengers hurried by to catch the trains that started every few minutes. Carriages drove up with their loads of ladies and children. Further down the street, porters unloaded express-wagons filled with freight and baggage with a large amount of noise and crash. Amongst all this confusion stood Daisy, opposite the door of the ladies' entrance.

The passers-by did not know she was a "Daisy," or that what she held so lovingly were her namesakes. Now and then a passer-by stopped to buy one of the five or ten cent bouquets. As they purchased a bouquet from her basket, most spoke a kind word to the child. Something in Daisy's look and manner pleaded for tenderness and sympathy.

The girl did not look like she belonged in the depot. Even in her homemade dress, she looked so dainty. She moved and spoke like a little lady. She appeared accustomed to a different kind of life. All who noticed her, or stopped to buy her flowers, hurried on. They had no time for more than a passing interest in the child. They contented themselves with wondering and pitying.

Down the street came a lady with a little girl. The little girl came skipping and jumping as she held her mother's hand. She felt happy and as full of play and merry pranks as any kitten. She had spent a pleasant day with her mother in the city. Now she was returning to her country home with lots to tell and many pretty purchases.

"Oh see, Mama!" she said, as her eye fell upon Daisy. "See those pretty flowers that little girl is selling. She is just about as large as Lola Swan. Doesn't she look nice and sweet? Won't you buy some flowers from her, Mama?"

"You have plenty of flowers at home, dear Lily. We have about as much as we can carry now," answered her mother.

"Oh Mama, those little bouquets will take up a tiny mite of room. I want you to buy some out of kindness to the little girl. Her eyes look so sad, Mama," said Lily.

Moved by the pleadings of her daughter, Mrs. Ward turned toward the flower-girl and asked the price of her bouquets.

"What a pretty pot of daisies! Can I have that, Mama?" asked Lily.

At this, Daisy drew back. She put one hand over the pot of daisies she held in the other hand. She looked as though she feared they would take the pot from her by force.

"I will ask Papa to carry them for me, Mama," said Lily.

"Ho! ho!" said a cheery voice behind her. "You think Papa has nothing better to do than turn express-man and carry your packages, do you? I wonder how many bundles wait for me in the depot to put safely in the cars." Lily turned about and saw her father, who had overtaken his wife and little girl.

"Oh, lots and lots!" said Lily, jumping about with glee as she saw him. "We bought something for everybody, Papa. I bought a present for your birthday tomorrow, but it is a secret. Mama will fill it with ink. I will put it on your desk before you come down in the morning. You won't ask what it is, will you?"

"No I won't," said Mr. Ward. "However, you must hurry and buy your flowers, or we will not find good seats in the cars. You want these daisies, do you? How much are they, my child?"

Again Daisy drew back. "I cannot sell them, Sir," she said. "At least not now, not if...."

"Oh, saved for some favorite customer, hey? You see, Lily, you cannot have them. Well, pick out your bouquets. We will hang them about our necks if we cannot carry them any other way," said Mr.

3

Ward. "This is the little girl I told you about, my dear," he said, turning to his wife.

Looking at the sweet, sad face of the young flower vendor, the lady asked, "What is your name, my child?"

"My name is... they call me Margaret," said the child with hesitation in her voice and manner. Her face had become flushed.

Mr. Ward, having paid for the flowers Lily had chosen, hurried his wife and daughter away. As they left he said to his wife, "There, my dear, I did not say too much about that child, did I?"

"Why no," said Mrs. Ward, looking back to the small figure standing beside the basket of flowers. "I find her very interesting. She has a strangely elegant manner and speech for one in her position. I wish we had time to talk more to her."

The flower-girl looked after them and sighed a long, weary sigh as she watched the playful Lily.

"Most all little girls have their fathers and mothers," she said softly to herself. "I do not have either. I wonder why God took both of mine away, but did not take me, too. Did He not know how lonesome I would become? I do not see what good I can do for Him when I am alone, except for Betty and Jack. However, God knows. Maybe He wants me to be patient until He's ready to take me."

The wistful eyes brightened again. After watching Lily and her parents disappear within the door of the depot, she turned the other way looking for new customers.

4

"There he comes," she said, as her eye fell upon a tall, broad-shouldered gentleman coming down the street. He had "soldier" written in every line and motion of his figure. His erect, stately head, down to the ringing tread of his firm foot, clearly revealed his military training.

"Good afternoon, little lady," he said. He returned her welcoming look with a pleasant smile. "Do you have my wife's bouquet all ready?"

Taking from the corner of her basket a larger bouquet made of choice flowers, she held it up to him.

"Thank you, Sir," she said, as she received the price. With her face flushed, she added, "Would it be too much trouble to carry this to the lady also?"

"Too much trouble? No! How much is it?" he said putting his hand again into his pocket.

"Oh! Sir! I did not mean that, I want to give the flowers for you to take to your lady. I want to send them to her because you treat me so kindly, and because... because you remind me of... of somebody."

"Well, I cannot refuse such a pretty gift, so prettily offered," said the gentleman. "Who do I remind you of?"

"My papa, Sir. You do look like him."

"Humph!" said the gentleman, not pleased at the idea that he looked like the father of this little, poor child.

"These are daisies, are they? My wife will like them."

5

"General, do you mean to miss the train?" said an acquaintance, as he passed.

"No, I certainly do not," said the gentleman. "I shall thank you for the lady tomorrow, my little girl."

As he turned to go, his foot slipped on a piece of orange-peel, thrown down by some careless person. Daisy caught his hand as he put it out. Her support, although frail and slight, steadied him.

The kind and generous soldier also had a quick temper. A fearful oath burst from his lips.

"Ah, my good angel, you saved me from a bad fall," he said almost in the same breath. He used a very different tone and manner as he turned to the child.

His good angel! Ah yes! More than he knew, his good angel. Those little hands would from this time hold him from falling back into the sin he had just committed.

Years ago, General Forster would never have allowed such words to escape his lips. Although even then, he did not speak carefully of sacred persons or things. In the bustle and excitement of war he, like many other brave men, had allowed himself to fall into a bad habit. He sometimes took the Lord's name in vain. The General often became careless before men when his quick temper got the better of him. However, he never or seldom used such words before women or children.

"Why, have I hurt you?" he asked, seeing with surprise her startled, troubled face.

6

"No Sir, oh no!" she answered, catching her breath, "but, but..."

"Well, but what?"

"But I am so sorry," she said. Distressed, she covered her face with her hands and burst into tears.

"Sorry for what?" he asked.

She gave him no answer but shrank a little away.

"Sorry for what?" he repeated as if determined to know. The tone of his command forced her to answer in instant obedience, whether she wanted to or not.

"Sorry for those words you said, Sir," she sobbed.

"Those words? What words?" His question answered itself as he spoke, for his forgotten words came back to him. He stood scolded before this poor little flower-girl. He repented from his heart, but only because he had upset this young child. He had not repented because he had offended the Holy One whose name he had profaned.

Puzzled, he said rather impatiently, "You mean to say that you never hear such words? Where you stand, rough men and boys mill about you all day long."

"Oh, yes, Sir!" she said, sorrowfully. "I do hear such words often. I try not to, but I cannot help it. It makes me sorry to hear them. I thought those poor men and boys did not know how to read. I thought perhaps they did not know what God said in

7

His commandments. I did not think gentlemen said such things; and I liked you so much."

Did she like him less now? He, the gentleman, the rich man, did not wish to lose the respect of this little child. He felt ashamed and sorry. He realized that the girl's innocent simplicity and truthfulness caused her to say what she did, not rudeness.

The good-hearted General acknowledged his wrong. "You are right, Margaret," he said. "Gentlemen should not say such things, especially before ladies and children. I forgot myself just then and behaved with bad manners."

She took her hands from her face and looked up at him. An unspoken question remained in her clear, earnest eyes. Plainly, she was not yet satisfied.

"Well," he said smiling at her, "what troubles you still? Let me have it all."

"I am wondering what difference could it make, Sir."

"What difference could what make?"

"Whether ladies or children heard it, Sir," she answered timidly. "God hears it all the same, doesn't He? It can't make any difference to Him who else hears it."

She looked up at the blue sky overhead as she spoke. The look and the words brought to him a sudden sense of God's presence and nearness. The General had known before that the Almighty Eye saw him always and that the Almighty Ear heard him always. However, he never felt it as he did now. The gentle, timid scolding had gone far deeper than the little giver had intended. Her hearer felt ashamed. He had confessed that he would pay a respect to a woman or child; a respect he did not feel the need to pay to his Maker. He could give her no answer.

"You behind time, General?" said the voice of another friend as he hurried past. The scream of the warning whistle told the gentleman that he had no time to lose.

"I'll see you tomorrow. Good-bye, my child. God bless you," he said hurriedly.

He rushed away just in time. As he boarded, the train started into motion. The jar threw him once more off his balance. The General caught the railing to save himself, while again hasty, improper words rose to his lips.

However, the improper words did not pass his lips. He checked the words before even the summer wind could catch them. In their place the angels carried up the heart felt prayer, "God keep me from uttering them in time to come."

The one seated next to him in the car thought General Forster remarkably silent and unsociable that afternoon. He would not talk but buried himself behind his newspaper. If the neighbor had looked closer, he would have seen the General's eyes not fixed on the paper. The General looked instead at the little pot of daisies which rested on his knee. Over the delicate pink and white blossom he breathed a vow; a vow registered in heaven and faithfully kept on earth.

Chapter 2

A CLUSTER OF DAISIES

"What are you thinking about, Frank?" asked Mrs. Forster. She looked at her husband as he stood leaning against the casing of the window. He gazed thoughtfully out at the lovely garden beyond.

"I am thinking about a bad habit of mine," he answered.

"You have none; at least none that I cannot put up with," she said playfully.

"That's not the question, dear Gertrude," he returned gravely. "It is whether my Maker can put up with it. I believe that He cannot. God has said He, '...will not hold him guiltless that taketh His name in vain.'"

Mrs. Forster colored as she bent her head over the sleeping baby on her lap.

"You did not know, perhaps," her husband said, after a minute's silence, "that I was ever guilty of this sin?"

"I did know it, Frank. I have heard you, now and then, when you spoke to your dogs or when you became a little impatient with the men. You did not mean me to hear such words. I noticed you never used them in my presence."

"No," he said a little sadly. "I would not speak in my wife's presence words unfit for her to hear. However, I forgot an ear still purer which I insulted and defied. I realized today, Gertrude, that I have treated the Almighty with less reverence and respect than I show my fellow man. Let me tell you of the lesson I received from the innocent little flower-girl who sent the daisies to you."

Sitting down beside her, he told her of the teaching which came to him from the little wayside blossom. They talked of the girl and her pretty, lady-like ways and sayings, which seemed so far above her station. They did not know she was a "Daisy," and that the flowers she sent were her namesake. As they talked, Mrs. Forster cried happy tears mingled with many a blessing for the little flower giver.

Plucking one of the flowers from the stem, she opened her baby's tiny hand and placed the flower within it. The little fingers clasped tight around it as the unconscious little one slept on.

"Her name is Gertrude, but we'll call her Daisy, Frank," said the young mother. "Her pretty nickname will remind us of the lesson learned today."

"You think I may forget?" said her husband, smiling. "I trust not. My little teacher plainly pointed out the sin and rudeness of taking God's name in vain. I must have a short memory, indeed, if I failed to remember her lesson. She thought gentlemen must know better."

"Dear," said the lady, "you said you would ask about the child and see if we could help her."

"So I did," he answered. "I should have done so before, but day after day I have let business or pleasure come first. I allow myself just enough time to catch the train and none to spend with the poor little creature. She seems so grateful for the few kind words I have given her. You think I am rather fanciful about this child, I know, Gertrude. I feel convinced that she has not always lived among the people who now surround her. I am not the only one of her customers who has noticed her grace. Ward and others have noted that her speech and manners are uncommon for a child of her class. However, like myself, they have never made it their business to look after her. Tomorrow I shall make sure to be at the depot in time to have a talk with her. I believe the child belongs to the woman who keeps the fruit stall at the corner. I wonder if she would give the child up and allow her to go to school."

The next morning, more than an hour earlier than usual, our little flower-girl saw "her gentleman." An eager, wistful little face, with some questioning fear in it, greeted him. She worried that she had offended her friend by her plain speech the day before.

The girl had not meant to speak so plainly. The gentleman's own questions drew the words from her. She now feared that he would think her rude and disrespectful.

She worried needlessly. His eye and voice had become even kinder than usual. As he came near to her, he laid his hand gently on her head. "Well, my little lady!" the General said. "How does the world go for you today? The lady told me to thank you very much for the daisies."

The young face brightened, "Did she like them, Sir?"

"Very much, in fact, she has a little one at home whom she plans to call Daisy after your pretty flowers."

"Is she your little girl, Sir?"

"Yes, she is a mite of a Daisy but a very precious one," he answered. He looked into the flushed face with its soft, shining eyes and added, "You are a Daisy yourself."

The flowers she held dropped at her feet unheeded. She clasped her hands and with filling eyes eagerly asked, "How did you know it, Sir? How did you know it?"

"Know what, my child? What troubles you?"

"How did you know I was Daisy?" she almost gasped.

"I did not know it," he answered in surprise. "Is your name Daisy? I thought it was Margaret."

"Betty and Jack call me Margaret, Sir. Daisy is my own name, that Papa and Mama called me," she answered, recovering herself a little.

"Where are your papa and mama?" he asked. "I thought the woman who keeps the fruit-stall at the corner was your mother."

16

"Oh no, Sir!" she said. "She is only Betty. She treats me well but she is not Mama. Mama was a lady," she added, with simple, childish dignity which told that she was a lady herself.

"Where are your father and mother?" he repeated, with fresh interest in the child.

"Mama drowned, Sir. We could never find Papa," she answered sadly.

"Come into the depot with me," said General Forster. "I want to talk to you."

She obeyed. Picking up her basket the girl followed him into the waiting room. Many curious eyes watched as he made her sit down beside him and he drew from her, her sad, simple story. She told of long ago when she had lived with Papa, Mama, her little brother, and baby sister in their own lovely home. Where it was, she did not know. It was a different place from the large bustling city where she now lived with Betty and Jack. She had left home with her mama and the baby on a large ship. She could not remember where they planned to travel. Betty was on board and Mama had treated her with kindness. A dreadful storm came and there was much confusion and terror. Then it seemed as if she went to sleep for a long, long time. She remembered nothing more until she found herself living with Betty and Jack in their poor home.

They nursed and cared for her during the many months she had been weak and sick. Now that she was stronger and better, she tried to help them all she could. She kept the two small rooms tidy while

17

Betty was away attending to her stall. In the afternoons, she sold flowers that Jack raised in his little garden and she arranged into bouquets. Finally, she told how from the very first time she saw General Forster, she thought he "looked so like Papa." The little girl told how happy she felt when he stopped to buy flowers and spoke kindly to her.

The girl told her story with a straightforward and simple sadness which went right to the listener's heart. The general had no doubt of its truth. The child could tell nothing of her own name or her parents' except that they called her "Daisy" at home. She had never since heard the familiar name until today when she thought this stranger had given it to her. Betty and Jack always called her Margaret. She loved daisies dearly for the sake of their name, which had been her own. She raised and tended, with loving care, the little plant she had given to "my gentleman." The daisies were given as a token of gratitude for his kindness and because he was "so like Papa."

Having learned all that he could from the child herself, the gentleman went to the fruit-woman on the corner.

"So," he said, "the little girl whom you call Margaret is not your own daughter?"

"Indeed not, Sir," answered Betty. "I never had a daughter of my own. Jack's not even mine but belonged to my sister who died. The likes of me would not be raising a little lady like her, unless she had none of her own to do it."

18

"Will you tell me how that came about?"

Betty told the story in as plain and simple a manner as the child's. Her husband had been steward on a sailing vessel running between New Orleans and New York. About three years ago, she had been allowed to go with him for the voyage. She was sick and the doctor had ordered a change of air, but the voyage made her worse instead of better. On the return trip she would have died, Betty declared, if Margaret's mother had not tenderly cared for her. Betty remembered the lady's name as Saacyfut, but Margaret said that was not right. The lady was on her way to New York with her sick little girl, a baby, and a French nurse. Her home was neither there nor in New Orleans, at least so the child afterwards said.

Her own account of the storm was the same as the child's. However, while the recollection of the little one could go no further, Betty remembered, only too well, the horrors of that day.

When the ship began to sink, all who were on board were trying to leave. There was much confusion. Betty sat in one lifeboat, the French nurse, with the child in her arms, beside her. The lady was about to follow with the infant when a mast fell, striking the Frenchwoman on the head and killing her instantly. The mast also knocked overboard one of the three sailors who were in the boat. At the same time, the boat parted from the ship and was at the mercy of the raging waves. In vain the two sailors remaining on the boat tried to regain the ship. The waves swept the boat farther and farther away and soon they lost sight of the vessel. They drifted about all night. The next morning a fishing vessel found them and brought them to New York.

Fright, exposure, and other hardships seemed to have cured Betty, but were too much for the poor little girl. She lay ill for months, too weak to move or speak. She appeared to have lost all memory and sense. When at last she grew better and stronger, her reason and recollection came back. However, she could not tell the name of her parents or her home.

"Margaret Saacyfut," Betty persisted in saying. The French nurse had called her "Mamsel Marguerite."

"Marguerite" had been the French woman's name for "Daisy", this the General saw plainly enough. However, he could make nothing of the surname.

"Did you not look for the child's family, Betty?" he asked.

"Indeed I did, Sir," she answered. "I even advertised her but all to no good. I wrote to New Orleans, to the ship owners, but they never bothered to even answer. It took a lot of money, Sir, to pay the paper. I couldn't look any longer. For you see, my man went down with the ship and was never heard of, along with the rest, to this day. I had to use up the bit he'd put by in the bank until the child mended enough for me to leave her with Jack."

"How generous of you to burden yourself with her care," said General Forster.

"Burden is it, Sir? Never was she a burden, the sweet lamb, not even when her sense had left her. My neighbors always asked why I didn't put her in the hospital. Why would I do that after her mother saved me from a burial in the sea? For sure if it had not been for the lady, I would have died on the ship and they'd chucked me overboard. Could I turn out her child after that? Isn't the child paying me for it now, earning her living and mine too? She and Jack tend the bit of a garden and afternoons she comes down and sells her flowers. Who has the heart to refuse her with her pretty ways and nice manners? She's a lady every inch of her, like her mother before her."

And thrusting her head out from her stall, Betty gazed down the street with admiring affection at her young friend.

"Oh! But she's the jewel of a child," she went on. "It is surprising how Jack and me improved and became refined along with her. You see, Sir, I used to say a lot of words that weren't right. I didn't mean them for swearing, but it was just a way of speaking. After Margaret began to mend and get about, you would have thought she was killed entirely if I let one out of my mouth. So seeing how it hurt her, I just minded what I said. Jack did the same for he was a boy that swore awful, poor fellow. He'd been left to himself and how was he to know better? At first we minded our tongues so that we wouldn't hurt the child. By and by she made it plain to us that it was the great Lord Himself that we offended. Knowing that she'd been taught better than me, I just heeded her. Now Sir, them words that I never thought no harm of and used to come so easy, I just leave them out of my speech. It sounds a great deal better and no doubt more pleasing to Him that's above. Jack does the same, mostly, although he does let one slip now and then. So you see, Sir, it's not a burden. She is, all in all, a bit of light and comfort to the house that holds her."

Glad to find a listener in a "gentleman the likes of him," Betty had talked away to the gentleman. So taken up with her story, she paid little heed to the business of her stall. She made wrong change more than once. She gave quarts instead of pints, oranges in place of apples, and provoked some impatient customers more than a little. One wicked boy, seeing her attention occupied with something else, ran off without paying for the popcorn he asked for.

However, Betty lost nothing by the time and thought she gave to the gentleman or the interest she showed in Margaret. The kind gentleman slipped money into her hand as he left. Money which the warm-hearted Irishwoman laid aside to buy that new dress and pair of shoes Margaret needed so badly.

Chapter 3

THE DAISY TRANSPLANTED

"Betty," said General Forster, stopping the next morning at the fruit-woman's stall, "could you give up that little girl; if you felt sure it was for her good?"

Betty sighed and shook her head mournfully as she answered. "I've always looked to give her up, Sir, if Saacyfuts, or whatever their name is, turned up. If it was for her good, never a word would they hear from me, although, Jack and me would feel bad. You're not telling me you've found her friends since last night, Sir?"

"Not the people she belongs to, certainly, Betty. I have found those who will become friends to her. If you will consent, they will provide for her. She should go to school and become well educated; do you not think so?"

"Indeed, none knows that better than myself, Sir. Is it yourself that's the friend you're speaking of?" Betty gave a searching look into the gentleman's face.

He smiled. "Yes," he said. "I would like to put her in school and take care of her. She seems to be a sweet child and a good one. You see Betty, I have it in my power to do more to find her friends than you are able to do. We may trace them yet. If we never find them, I will promise to provide for her as long as it may be necessary. Are you willing?"

Betty again stared into the face of the General as if she would look him through. "I am sensible of your kindness, Sir," she answered. "You see, I'm in a way responsible for the child. I'd say yes and thank you kindly, but... you'll excuse my plain speaking... you're a stranger to me. I could not part with Margaret unless I was certain of your character. For if I didn't think she would be brought up right, never a step would she go with you. I saw Miss Gertrude Allston walking with you once last summer, Sir, just after I set up my stand here. She never noticed me. I used to be laundrywoman in her mother's house before I married. Miss Gertrude was a sweet and good child as you're saying of Margaret. She'll never go far wrong, I'm sure of that. You just bring me a line from her and if she says you're all right, I'll not say no."

General Forster laughed heartily, not a bit offended at Betty's plain speaking. "Miss Gertrude Allston, as you call her, will give me all the lines you want, Betty. She thought me right enough to marry me. She is my wife."

"Is it so, Sir?" said Betty, dropping the rosy apple she held. She gazed at the gentleman with a mixture of curiosity and admiration that was amusing to see. "If Miss Gertrude manages you, that is character enough. I'll say take the child and my blessing on all of you. When she gets among you fine folks, you'll not let her forget the woman who cared for her when there was no one else to do it, will you, Sir? You will let me see her once in a while?"

The General readily promised this and went on to tell Betty what plans he and his wife had for Daisy. First, she would go for a while to his home where Mrs. Forster would provide her with proper clothing. Then they would send her to Miss Collins' boarding school. Miss Collins would teach and train her in a way that would satisfy her family if they should ever find her. Daisy would also have training so she could someday earn her own living if necessary.

"I'm glad she will have the bringing up of a lady. I couldn't give her that," said Betty with another sigh. Her heart hurt to part with her darling. "She cannot become more of a lady than she is now, even if you dress her in jewels, silks, and satins. Never a rough word nor way about her in the two years she has spent with Jack and me. You could not find a prettier behaved child in all the land."

An hour or two later, Betty found a friend to watch her stall for her. She guided General Forster to the tiny house in the suburbs of the city where she lived with Daisy and Jack.

The two children were in the garden gathering flowers for the bouquets Daisy sold. They looked up when they heard the gate open. The children expressed surprise to see Betty home at this unusual hour and to see the gentleman with her. Daisy flushed and smiled with delight upon hearing what the gentleman, who looked so like Papa, planned for her. However, the little face shadowed over and she shook her head gently but firmly when asked if she would go.

"And why not, dear?" asked Betty. "Surely, you will not throw away a chance like this."

Daisy shook her head again. Then first begging the gentleman's pardon, she stepped up to her faithful friend. She put her arms about her neck and whispered something in her ear.

The tears Betty had kept back with trouble, now came to her eyes. "Oh, is that it, honey?" she said. "Don't let that trouble your dear heart. What a tender, grateful little soul you are." While she lovingly soothed the little girl, Betty went on, "You see, Sir, it's just as I said. She is a lady, every inch of her. There's a matter of back rent due, although my landlord is good as gold, and other bills with the druggist, baker, and the grocery man. I've never caught up since the child was sick. She says she won't leave now that she can help by selling her flowers.

Drawing the child to him, General Forster whispered to her. He promised to pay the back rent and bills if she would come with him. Daisy, feeling nearer to home and friends than anytime since the dreadful day of the shipwreck, put her hand trustingly in his.

The parting went hard. Daisy could not leave those kind friends, who shared their little with her, without sad tears. Betty kissed and clung to her. She pronounced God's blessings upon her. Jack hung over the gate, uttering frantic howls as he watched the sobbing child led away by her new protector. Jack gave no thought to the other boys who flocked to see what ailed him. They admired Jack because he was bigger, stronger, and braver than any other boy of his age among the group. He was also their terror. He allowed no bad word to be used in his presence, banishing from their games all who offended him. He chose as his favorites and chief companions those who were careful not to take God's name in vain. One heard cursing and swearing less frequently among the lanes and lots lying around the humble house. Daisy had bloomed and grown during the two years she lived there. Unknown to her, she planted her good seed upon the path which God chose for her.

Betty went back to her stand with a sad heart. She knew when she went home that night she would miss the sweet little face. Daisy had brightened and cheered her after many a hard day's work. She felt half-consoled for her own loss when she saw Daisy coming down the street holding General Forster's hand. The General had taken the little girl to a store and bought her new clothes. However, Daisy was as much a lady in the coarse, but clean, calico frock she had worn yesterday as she was in the new clothes. The sweet manners and pretty ways she had never lost made her a lady. The new garments covered as warm and loving a little heart as the old ones had done. Betty knew that pride would have no place in Daisy's heart. As she reached the stand, Daisy ran behind the stall and threw her arms about Betty's neck. She kissed her again and again as lovingly as she had when she had no other friend in the world.

Gentle Mrs. Forster gave Daisy a warm welcome to her new home. The child fell at once into the ways and habits of those about her, plainly showing they were not new to her. She had at some time lived differently from the way she had lived for the past two years.

She had charming ways of her own and showed dainty grace in her speech and behavior. The little girl cared for others with a thoughtfulness that was surprising in a child of her age. Daisy, no older than about eight, had received careful training at one time. The lessons learned had taken deep root, not forgotten in spite of the long separation from her home and family.

The Forsters had intended to send the little girl to boarding school at Miss Collins'. However, she soon grew so close to the hearts of her new friends that they could not bear to part with her. For the present, at least, they decided that their home would become hers. Daisy would go to Miss Collins for the morning, as most of the other little girls in Glenwood did.

Mrs. Forster could not bear to send this loving child from her. Daisy's greatest happiness seemed to be in making others happy. She grew more and more interesting every day. The familiar objects and customs about her called up past recollections of the home and parents she had lost. She would watch the General for hours at a time as he sat reading or writing. She followed him with wistful eyes as he mounted his horse and rode down the broad avenue, just like Papa. The little girl hung over the smaller Daisy as she lay sleeping, because "she looks as our baby at home used to." She delighted to wait upon her and Mrs. Forster in a neat-handed manner. Loving service came naturally to her.

She never called the infant, "baby," as the rest of the family did. With her it was always "little Daisy." She seemed to love the pretty name, whether given to herself or another. All the variety of choice flowers which filled the Forster's garden could not win her affection from her old favorite. Daisies remained her favorite "because Mama loved them so and named me after them."

Although she remembered so much, the child could not recall the name of her parents or where they had lived. Their name "was not what Betty called it," she was sure; but none the less it had passed from her mind.

Francine, the French maid, called Daisy's mama, "Madam," and Daisy, "Mademoiselle Marguerite." When asked what other people used to call mama and papa, the little face grew clouded and pained with the effort to remember. When they mentioned name after name to her, she shook her head at each one.

The General tried by every means in his power to discover the girl's family. He knew that they must still mourn the loss of their sweet little daisy blossom. As week after week went by, he and his wife decided unless her relations came to claim her, she would stay with them. She was an added ray of light where all had been brightness and sunshine before. Daisy was a lovely, precious little flower, lending new fragrance and beauty to the home where she blossomed.

Chapter 4

DAISY'S SISTER FLOWERETS

"I didn't mean to, Susy; 'pon my word and honor I didn't; just as sure as I'm alive."

Holding General Forster's hand, Daisy heard the two voices as she approached Miss Collins' garden. Today was her first morning of school.

From the sounds of the exclamation of the first speaker one would think some terrible misfortune had happened. The second speaker thought herself accused of some dreadful crime and that she must prove her innocence. And what had happened? Why just this....

Susy Edwards and several of her schoolmates were making the land of Egypt. The young class studied Egypt in geography. The pictures of pyramids and the sphinx fascinated the children. So during their play time Susy proposed that they turn a portion of their playground into Egypt. The children spent recess of the day planning and building. Having left their project with regret, they returned to it before school time the next morning.

The gravel walk represented the desert; the trough which led the waste water from the spring, the Nile River. A jointed wooden doll, cruelly deprived for the purpose, of all its limbs and buried halfway in the gravel, represented the Egyptian statue. Construction on pyramids, four or five inches high and built of pebbles, was in progress.

The pyramids neared completion; the little builders expecting each moment to hear the bell. Lola Swan came with a fresh supply of pebbles. As she hurried, she tripped over a stick which lay upon the grass. Trying to recover herself, her load fell around and upon the half-built pyramid. Not much harm was done, knocking only a few stones from it. However, Susy immediately exclaimed...

"Goodness gracious! Mercy me!" Lola answered, as you heard. Their words met Daisy's ear as she and General Forster entered the garden.

The click of the gate-latch caused all the children to look up. The sight of the new scholar made them forget the pyramids for the moment.

"Why, there's Daisy Forster!" said Lily. Daisy was now known by this name.

"I wonder if she's coming here to school," said another. That question speedily became answered.

The General stopped by the group and said, "Here's a new schoolmate for you. Will you treat her kindly and make her feel at home?"

They all knew and liked the General. "Yes Sir, we will. I'll take care of her," said Lily. She scrambled to her feet, taking Daisy's hand in a patronizing manner. "She won't feel a stranger after one day. We'll all be good to her and she can help us make our land of Egypt."

"Ah! That is what you are doing, is it?" said the General.

"Yes Sir," answered Lily. "We're just putting up a pyramid. Lola knocked part of it down. She didn't mean to."

With the bell now ringing, the little group turned toward the house. Daisy wondered how a matter so easily settled could call for such violent expressions of distress and alarm as she had heard.

"Why Miss Collins," said General Forster, as she met them at the door, "what a bouquet of flowers you have here! A Rose, a Violet, a Daisy, and a Lily; as choice a bunch of flowers as one could wish for."

"And the Lily is going to take care of the Daisy and make her feel at home, Miss Collins," said Lily. "The General said I could."

"No, he didn't," said Susy.

"Yes, he did, upon my word he did. At least, I said I would do it. He didn't say I couldn't; did you, Sir?" said Lily. She threw back her head to look up at the General's tall figure.

"And that comes to the same thing, does it, Lily?" he said, laughing. "Well, I suppose it does. I promise, you shall look after Daisy until she feels no longer a stranger among you."

"She knows Lola, Violet, and I as well as anything," said Lily. The little girls had met several times before. Lily felt herself and the two Swans to be on rather close terms with Daisy Forster.

"All right then. I leave her to you. Good morning, Miss Collins," he said, with a bow to the lady. Kissing Daisy and nodding pleasantly to the little ones, he went away.

Daisy felt rather lonely when he left, in spite of Miss Collins' kind look. Lily tightly clasped her hand and Violet said, "We have real nice times in school. Don't be afraid." Daisy felt far shyer with children than with grown people, probably because she never had any companions her own age. The number of young faces about her, most of them strange, made her long to be back at Mrs. Forster's side. And they all looked at her a good deal, for they knew her story well. She was an object of great curiosity.

Lily saw this as she took her seat with Daisy beside her. She thought she must speak up for her charge. "Miss Collins," she said, "please, make a rule."

"Well," said Miss Collins, smiling. Lily constantly asked for new rules concerning things which did not suit her. She had begun with this more than a year ago when she was only a visitor at the school. Even now, she was not a regular scholar but only a student for a few weeks. Her papa and mama had gone on a journey. Lily felt lonely at home when Ella and the boys attended school. Her parents had arranged for Lily to go with Ella to school in the mornings. She was rather a privileged person and spoke her mind freely on matters which did not please her. The other children thought her rules

36

rather a joke but usually they followed her requests. So now they all listened.

"Please make a rule that nobody can stare, Ma'am," said Lily. "It makes people feel so bad to be stared at," ...and Lily put up both hands to her cheeks..., "especially if they are new."

"Very true," answered Miss Collins. "Let us all try to remember the Golden Rule. Then we shall neither stare nor do anything else to hurt another's feelings."

Then she struck the little bell which stood upon her table. All knew that school had begun and they must become quiet.

Next, calling Bessie Norton to her, Miss Collins gave her a number of Bibles. The little girl handed one to each of her classmates. Then Miss Collins read a verse aloud and the children followed each in her turn.

"Minnie Grey may take the Bibles," said Miss Collins when they had finished their reading.

Minnie rose and began collecting the Bibles. Instead of taking a few at one time and coming back for the rest, she piled one on top of another. With her arm overloaded with books, Minnie came to Daisy and held out her other hand for Daisy's book. As she did so, the top one of the pile fell to the floor. Minnie stooped for it and down went two or three more.

"Oh! Bother the old things," said Minnie, in a low, impatient voice.

Daisy stooped to help her pick up the Bibles. However, bending over did not cause the glow her cheeks wore when she raised her head again.

Bother the old things! What old things? Why, the Bibles, God's own Holy Word. Daisy felt shocked and she looked up at Miss Collins. She expected to hear her reprove such wicked words.

Miss Collins had not heard Minnie's exclamation, although the noise of the falling books called her attention that way. She said, "Minnie, my dear, do not treat those Bibles carelessly. Do you forget who the Books belong to?"

"I don't care," muttered Minnie, but not so the lady could hear. Daisy heard again. The thought passed through her mind, "What a wicked little girl Minnie must be!"

Yet, Daisy was mistaken. If she asked Minnie's parents, teacher, or playmates, they all would tell her Minnie behaved well. A pleasant little girl, Minnie acted obediently and truthfully. She always tried to help others. She had no thought now that she had broken one of God's commandments. Minnie would have felt offended and grieved had she known the thoughts in Daisy's mind. She believed herself innocent of any wrong.

Chapter 5

DAISY: A STUDY

Daisy soon felt at home with the schoolmates and became a favorite among them.

It was not surprising that the children liked and became interested in her. She was such a gentle, modest, amiable little girl. Daisy watched and joined in the games and lessons of the others with an innocent wonder which amused and touched them. For Daisy was not at all accustomed to playing with children of her own age. Their ways were all new to her.

Of course, Daisy was behind all the rest in her studies. She could not even read as well as Lily Ward. She began with the simplest lessons, such as Lily and two or three of the youngest children learned. At first, this troubled her. She feared the rest of the class would laugh at her.

Daisy soon found she need not worry of that. The law of kindness ruled in Miss Collins' young class. The little girls would have thought it a crime to laugh or mock Daisy for what was not her fault.

They might, now and then, disagree a little among themselves, for they were by no means perfect children. Sometimes one showed some selfishness or even a few angry words passed from one to another. However, they usually agreed about as well as any twenty little girls could. Not one among them purposely did unkind things to another, least of all to Daisy. Because of her sad and colorful history, they all looked upon Daisy with a tender pity and interest. Like Lily, Daisy became a pet with both the teacher and students. They encouraged and aided her as much as possible.

So Daisy found plenty of helpers who, far from laughing at her mistakes, thought her quick and industrious. Indeed, she tried hard to make up for lost time and catch up with those of her own age.

She was almost too eager about catching up. The long illness which followed the shipwreck had left Daisy weak. Too much study or play over-tired the little girl and made her nervous and sick. Her little head would become confused and ache. Now and then Mrs. Forster would have to take the books from her and forbid more study. She would send her out to play or to work in the plot of ground that was Daisy's own garden. Not always pleased at this, Daisy sometimes became fretful and impatient. Mrs. Forster soon found a way to put a stop to this.

One afternoon she found the little girl bending over her slate with flushed and heated cheeks, anxious eyes, and trembling hands. "Daisy," she said quietly, "What are you doing? Miss Collins has not given you lessons out of school, has she?"

"No, Ma'am," said Daisy. "I asked Ella Ward to give me math problems so I could do them at home. I can't make this one come out right. I know it is not right, because Ella put the answers on the other side of the slate. No matter what I do, mine will not come out the same."

"This sum is too hard for you, Daisy," she said. "You do not know enough arithmetic for this."

"Lola, Violet, and the other girls my age do problems as hard as that," answered Daisy. She looked ready to burst out crying. "I have to do arithmetic with the very little ones, like Lily. I feel so ashamed, so I want to go on to the harder ones. Please, give me the slate again, Aunt Gertrude," she added, as Mrs. Forster laid it beyond her reach.

"No, dear. I do not wish you to study out of school. I am glad you want to improve, but you have as much to do there as is good for you. At home, I want you to rest and play. You are improving rapidly. However, for a time you must feel content to go on with those who are younger than yourself."

"But it makes me ashamed," pleaded Daisy again.

"There is no reason for that," said Mrs. Forster, patting the hot cheek Daisy raised towards her. "The other children do not laugh at you and make you uncomfortable, do they?"

"Oh no, Ma'am," said Daisy. "They all treat me well, but they can't help see what a dunce I am." Daisy's tears overflowed as she went on. "They always say kind things about how I never went to school before and how my own dear mama drowned. They know nobody taught me until I came to you."

"You are not a dunce, dear," said the lady. "A child who idles away her time and cares not whether she learns is a dunce. A little girl who really wishes to be industrious but does not know quite as much as others her age is not a dunce. God has not given you the same advantages as the other girls in time past. No one will think my Daisy a dunce. Now, we must do no more studying at home, no more lessons than those Miss Collins gives you."

Daisy did not look satisfied. In fact, she even pouted a little.

"Daisy," said Mrs. Forster, "suppose Uncle Frank gave you a beautiful and costly gift, like a watch which would become useful to you at a later time, if you took care of it. What would you do with it?"

"Why, I would take good care, oh, such care of it!" said Daisy. She widened her eyes in surprise at the question. She did not see what that could have to do with her studies. "I'd wind it up every night and keep it safe every way I could; although, I don't know if I am quite old enough to have and care for a watch of my own. Maybe I would ask you or Uncle Frank to keep it for me until I became older."

"Suppose, for a while, he gave you no key to this watch but let it run down and be quiet?"

"I'd just patiently put it away until he gave me a key," said Daisy, wondering more and more.

"If, by and by, when he gave you this key, would you wind and wind the watch until the wheels and springs all broke? If you did, would Uncle Frank think you cared much for his gift?"

"Why no, Aunt Gertrude, he wouldn't think I cared much for him either if I misused his beautiful present."

"You are right, dear. Now, I want my own little Daisy to see how it is with herself. God gave you a young mind, bright and quick enough. For awhile, He did not choose that it should do much work. Now, He has given you the key by which you may wind and set it to work. If you hurt and wear out this precious gift, would it not seem as if you cared very little about it? Would it not seem that you did not respect and honor the Giver?"

"Yes'm," answered Daisy, beginning to see what Mrs. Forster meant, "but I never thought about that."

"I believe I never thought about it before, dear," said Mrs. Forster, smiling. "I am not afraid to praise you, Daisy. I have never seen any little child who showed such true honor and reverence for her Maker and all which belongs to Him. Someone taught you well, my child. For you to know and remember such lessons is worth all the book learning in the world."

Daisy felt pleased when anyone spoke to her of her long-lost home. She felt pleased to hear the teaching, which she received from those who had cared for and loved her, praised.

From this time on, there was no further trouble about the lessons. For Daisy had no desire to misuse any one of God's good gifts. Those older and wiser than herself had learned many a good lesson from Daisy. They learned from the little one's loving care and respect to her Creator's name and to all the works of His hand.

The careless way in which many of her schoolmates used sacred names troubled Daisy. They did not mean any harm. They did not think it any sin. Every day Daisy felt shocked and distressed when hearing such words as "mercy," "gracious," "goodness," "good heavens," and the like. It had become a habit with nearly all the school children. One caught it from another almost without knowing it. Lily Ward once thought the Pastor preached a sermon at her, because she said "hush up" now and then. Now, she followed the example of the others when anything puzzled or surprised her. A few weeks at school had accustomed Lily to the use of expressions which a year ago she would have considered naughty words.

The older girls in Miss Sarah Collins' room had fallen into this bad habit as much, if not more, than the younger class.

Daisy also thought it strange that they could handle the Bible, God's holy Word, with so little reverence and respect. They knocked the Bible about with their other books as if it were no better than the others. Sometimes they even used the Bible for uses that no book, even common ones, should suffer.

Daisy wondered why Miss Collins did not teach them better. Either she did not notice all this, or she did not think it important. Certainly, she did not correct them and the evil seemed to Daisy to grow worse from day to day.

At first, she did not like to speak out herself. You may wonder why, since she had not feared to speak so plainly to General Forster, a grown gentleman. However, she had done that almost without knowing what she said. His profane words had startled her so that he became surprised at her reaction. He had almost forced her to tell him what had disturbed her.

Here she was with everything strange around her; school, schoolmates, and teacher all new to her. It is not astonishing that she felt rather shy and afraid to tell others that she thought they behaved wrongly. By and by there came a day when she could no longer hold her peace.

Chapter 6

DAISY: A TEACHER

One morning just after school started, a heavy shower came up. When the time for the younger class' recess came, the wet ground forced the little ones to find amusement indoors.

"What shall we play?" asked Rosie Pierson.

"Lady Queen Fair," said Bessie Norton. "We'll go out on the porch and play it."

"Yes," said Violet. "Lily shall be Lady Queen Fair and we'll dress her up a little." Miss Emily, who gave music lessons to the girls, passed by. Violet asked her, "May we have a rose to put in Lily's hair for Lady Fair?"

The young lady smiled, stopped, and pulled a couple of roses from the vine which wound itself around a porch pillar. She gave them to Violet and then passed on.

In time past, Violet would have hoped or perhaps asked to be Lady Fair herself. Then she would have pouted and acted displeased if the other children had not agreed. Now, she was very different and more apt to prefer another before herself. The girls quickly arranged the roses, the one in the hair, the other in the collar of the little Lady Queen's blouse. Meanwhile, some of the other children drew forward one of the rustic chairs on the porch to serve as a throne.

The little queen, like many another royal lady before her, found her throne by no means an easy one. "Ow!" she said, rubbing her shoulders where she had scratched them against the rough bark on the back of the chair. "Ow! This is not nice at all or comfortable. My feet don't come to the floor and if I lean back I'm all scratched. I'd rather be a queen without a throne."

"Oh no! You must have a throne," said Susy Edwards. "Queens have to."

"I don't see why," said Lily rather grumpily. She did not feel very well that morning and the rainy day made her more fretful than usual. "I should think queens could do as they pleased and make their subjects do it, too. I don't see why they have to have their skin all scraped up, if they don't want to." Lily twisted her head to give a grieved look at the little fat shoulder with that red mark upon it.

"I'll fix you," said Lola. "I'll put Miss Collins' footstool under your feet and the big cushion behind you. Someone bring the cushion while I carry the stool." The girls brought the footstool in a moment, but they could not find the cushion.

"The big girls had it yesterday," said Fanny Satterlee. "I saw them with it during their recess when I went home. Here comes Cora Prime now; let's ask her. Cora, what did the big girls do with that cushion yesterday when they finished with it?"

"The Lord knows, I don't," said Cora, playfully tapping Fanny on the head with the roll of music in her hand.

"Oh!" exclaimed Lily.

Daisy did not speak. As Cora's eye happened to fall upon her, Daisy's face said as much as Lily's "Oh!"

"What's the matter with you two?" asked Cora, looking with good-nature from one to the other of the little girls.

"You oughtn't say that," said Lily.

"Ought not to say what?"

"The Lord knows," answered Lily.

"Well, doesn't He know?" asked Cora.

"No," said Lily, doubtfully, "I guess not. I don't believe He'd bother Himself with knowing about a worn-out cushion that has a hole in the cover."

"Yes, He does, too," said Cora, laughing. "Are not the very hairs of our head numbered?"

"Now, I know you talked shamefully," said Lily.

You're talking Bible. That is not right, is it, Daisy?"

"No," said Daisy, as boldly as Lily herself spoke. Quoting scripture in a careless manner was also a habit of many in the school.

"You two saucy monkeys! Correcting your elders," said Cora, much amused. "I heard you both talking Bible to Miss Collins this morning with the rest of your class."

"We only said what we learned in Sunday school yesterday," said Lily. "That's not the same thing. I know it's not right to talk Bible that kind of way. Papa says so and he tells us not to do it."

"Your papa saying so does not make a thing right or wrong," said Cora.

"Yes, it does, too!" said Lily. "My papa knows a whole lot and he wouldn't tell a story for anything. Cora, you'd better go to your music lesson. I expect Miss Emily wants you."

"Oh, you are very considerate for Miss Emily all at once," said Cora, more amused than ever. "You haven't told me why I shouldn't say, 'the Lord knows,' when He does know."

Lily looked at Daisy, who stood by the arm of her chair, for help. The little one felt that Cora was wrong, but she did not exactly know how to answer. She had noticed how carefully Daisy honored the name of God.

"Is it not taking the name of God in vain?" said Daisy.

"Upon my word!" said Cora. "Do you mean to call that swearing?"

"Well yes," said Lily, taking up the word, "...a kind of baby swearing, I suppose. You know, it's not very good of you, Cora."

"Everybody says such things. They don't mean anything," said Cora.

"Not everybody," answered Lily. "Daisy doesn't."

"Then Daisy's uncommonly good," said Cora.

"Yes, she is," replied Lily. "I suppose everybody should behave uncommonly good and never say them."

Cora laughed again. "Everybody must mind their P's and Q's before you, mustn't they, Lily?" and away she ran to her music lesson.

"Here's the cushion," said Rosie Pierson, running out from the schoolroom. "I found it in the closet under the shelf. I suppose that's where those careless big girls left it."

They placed the cushion behind Lily's shoulders. Still the little queen fidgeted on her throne and declared she felt uncomfortable. "Because if I lean back against the cushion, my feet won't touch the stool," she said.

"We'll put something else on the stool to make it higher," said Nettie Prime, trying to arrange Lily satisfactorily. "What shall we take? Oh, I know. Daisy, run and bring the big Bible off Miss Collins' table for Lily to put her feet on."

Daisy, who made a motion to start forward as Nettie began to speak, stood still when she heard what she called for.

"Make haste," said the latter, impatiently. "We won't have a bit of time to play."

Daisy did not move but stood with rising color, trying to make up her mind to speak.

"Oh! You disobliging thing!" said Violet, and she ran for the book.

"Oh! Don't," said Daisy, as Violet came back and stooped to put the Bible on the footstool. "I didn't mean to act unhelpful, but we ought not to use the Bible to play with."

"Pooh!" said Violet, "Lily's little feet won't hurt it. It's all worn out anyway. The cover is real shabby."

"I didn't mean that," answered Daisy. "I meant because it is God's book, and we ought to treat it very carefully."

"Oh, fiddle! How awfully particular you are, Daisy," said Minnie Grey. "Why girls, do you know the other day when I played paper-dolls with her and I turned up a Bible to make the side of a house, she took it away. I put it back again, because it stood up better than the other books. She said she wouldn't play if I did so with the Bible."

"I suppose Daisy would call that taking God's name in vain," said another, half reproachfully. "Wouldn't you, Daisy?"

"I think it is something the same," answered Daisy. She felt as if all the others found fault with her. She felt they thought her "awfully particular," a label which no little girl likes.

"I don't see how," said Lola. "I know we ought not to play with the Bible; but I don't see how it is taking God's name in vain."

"The Bible is God's book. He told it to the men who wrote it. His name is in it many times," said Daisy. "I think it seems like taking His name in vain to play with it or to put things upon it or to knock it about like our other school-books. And it is not right to say 'the Lord knows,' and 'mercy,' and 'gracious,' and such words, when we are just playing or feel provoked."

"What is the harm?" asked Rosie. "'Mercy' and 'gracious' are not God's name."

"Well, no," said Daisy, slowly, not exactly knowing how to explain herself. "And maybe I make a mistake; but it does seem to me as if it was a kind of... of...."

"Of little swearing, as Lily says," said Lola.

"Yes," said Daisy. "Rosie thinks it is no harm. Even if it is not much harm, I don't see any good in it. We can talk as well without saying such words."

"I guess they are pretty wicked," said Lily. "The day Mama went away, I said 'good heavens.' She said, 'Lily! Lily!' very quick like she does when I do something very naughty. She asked me where I learned that. I told her Elly said it. I didn't mean to tell a tale about Elly. Mama looked sorry and she told me never to say it again. I guess mercy is almost the same. I guess I won't say it anymore. Daisy, if I hear the other girls say those words, I'll help you correct them."

Lily promised this with an air of such grave importance that the other children laughed. Not in the least abashed, Lily went on, "Papa's coming home day after tomorrow. I'll ask him to tell me a whole lot about God's name and why it is wrong to say those things. Then I'll tell all you girls. But I'm not coming to school anymore when Mama comes home; so you'll have to come to my house. I'll have a swearing class and teach you all about it."

Others might take Lily's words with a different meaning than what she intended. However, her schoolmates understood her and that was enough.

"Daisy," said Lola, "how do you know so much about these things when you don't know a lot about everyday lessons? You didn't even have anyone to teach you for a long time."

"I don't know," said Daisy. "I think my own mama taught me in the home I used to have." A dreamy look came into her eyes as she spoke of her far-away home and those she had loved there. "I think I've forgotten a good many things," she added. "Although, I couldn't forget what Mama taught me about Jesus and what He wanted us to do if we loved Him. I think if we do love Him we will respect words about His name, His heaven, or anything that is His. We will use them only in a good and gentle way."

"You are so very particular, Daisy," said Minnie. "I think you are most too particular."

"You can't become too particular about doing what Jesus likes," said Daisy.

The other children had all gathered around Daisy. They listened with interest to what she said. Perhaps, they heard her with more patience than they would give to anyone else. They looked upon her as a sort of fairy or princess in disguise; they thought of Daisy as a mystery. They thought of her as a storybook child, as Lily had described her when speaking of her at home.

"No," said Lola, thoughtfully, "but it does not seem as if such little things are wrong. I know it isn't right to play with the Bible or say its words when we joke; but I don't see the harm of saying 'goodness' or 'mercy' or 'heavens.' They are not God's name and I don't see how we take it in vain saying them."

Daisy looked thoughtful. She felt she was right and wanted to explain herself. She also felt shy and could not find words to do so.

Lily, whom shyness never troubled, came to her aid. "Never mind," she said. "I'll ask Papa as soon as he comes home. He'll tell us all about it. If he says it is naughty, why it is, and we won't do it. If he says it's good enough, why we will. That's the way to fix it." Here the bell rang.

"There now," said Susy Edwards, "we have to go in. We've wasted all our time talking and never had a bit of fun during recess."

However, Susy was mistaken. They all gained more good from their talk than they could have from any amount of play. Their discussion had set more than one young mind thinking. From this day, even the most careless among them would check themselves when she found herself using these words.

Chapter 7

THE SWEARING CLASS

Lily felt so happy when her papa and mama came home. She had so much to hear and to talk about that she forgot to ask her father to teach her about the third commandment. Besides, she no longer went to school. Her mother taught her at home as she had done before going on her journey. Not being in school, Lily did not hear or say those careless words which Daisy Forster had said it was not right to use.

The talk she and her friends had had came to mind one evening as the family all sat at the table.

"Mama," said Ella, "will you let Lily and me have a tea-party tomorrow? I want to ask half a dozen of our girls. I suppose Lily would like to have a few of the little ones at the same time."

"Yes," answered Mrs. Ward, "you may each ask six of your friends."

"Can Walter and I ask some of the fellows?" asked Ned.

"Oh mercy, no!" said Ella. "We don't want any boys. We're not having a regular party, Ned. I just want the girls to spend the afternoon. It makes more fuss to have boys, too."

"Goodness me! You needn't get into such a way about it," said Ned.

"Children," said Lily, "you needn't either of you swear about it." Her brother's and sister's words brought back to her what Daisy had said.

Lily's family generally considered her efforts to keep the family straight as a good joke. They usually received her reproofs and advice with a laugh. This time they felt her plain speaking too much. Ned exclaimed, "Well, who is swearing, I'd like to know? And who gave you permission to correct your elders?"

"Nobody, I just took it," said shameless Lily. Then turning to her father, she exclaimed, "Papa, I believe the girls in our school are pretty heathen. They don't know enough about the commandments. So I told them we'd have a swearing class and I'd ask you to teach it. You know a good deal about swearing. Tomorrow when they come, we can have our swearing class."

This speech turned the anger of Ella and Ned into amusement. They laughed with the others.

"I don't believe your playmates will thank you for asking them here for play and then bringing them up for a lecture from me, my pet," said Mr. Ward.

"Yes, they will Papa. They want to know about it. I think we'd better make a swearing party of this. I believe it would do those big girls good, too. They swear something dreadful. They don't seem to think they do, at least Cora doesn't. Mama, let's make a rule we won't have any swearing in this house; won't you?"

"Certainly," said Mama smiling. "First, we must find out what swearing is and then become careful not to break the rule."

"If one is going to call 'goodness' and 'mercy' and such things swearing, one might as well give up talking altogether," said Ella.

"Perhaps not only swearing," said her father, "the use of them is a bad habit. A very bad habit the young people of this place use too frequently. I notice it growing stronger, too, as all such habits do, going from bad to worse. I must go; I have not the time to talk to you about it now. If Lily can persuade her little friends to take the "swearing class" as part of their afternoon's entertainment, well and good. If not, we will have a little private talk among ourselves some other time."

Lily's proposal did not please Ella at all. She hoped that it would pass from the child's mind before the afternoon came. She carefully did not use any words that would remind Lily of her lecture.

This nearly proved successful. In the excitement of arranging her doll-house, setting out the new tea-set Mama had brought her, and dressing the doll which Papa had brought, Lily almost forgot her plan.

Her friends sat around a small table playing with the new china set, when Minnie said, "I have a secret to tell all of you if you'll promise never to tell."

"I won't," said Violet.

"On your sacred word and honor?" said Minnie.

"On my sacred word and honor," repeated Violet.

"And you, Rosie?" asked Minnie.

"On my word and honor," said Rosie.

"Sacred?" said Minnie.

"Sacred! Sacred word and honor," was Rosie's answer.

Lily repeated the words as desired and next came Daisy's turn.

"I won't tell," she said, when Minnie looked at her.

"On your sacred word and honor?" asked Minnie.

"I promise I won't tell, Minnie."

"But you must say on your word and honor."

"I can't," said Daisy.

"Then I won't tell you; and you're real mean, Daisy Forster," said Minnie. "Why won't you say so?"

"I don't see why I need to. I don't know if it is quite right," answered Daisy, coloring.

"Oh, Daisy Forster, what a girl you are!" said Rosie.

"Well," said Lily, "there's nothing left, except these two caramels. Daisy, you eat up this, and Bessie, you eat up the other. Now, the tea party is all done. We'll go and ask Papa about that commandment. He's playing croquet with the big girls, but they seem to be resting now."

Lily was right. The older girls had persuaded Mr. Ward to join in a game of croquet. He was a favorite among the young people in Glenwood. His presence never put a damper upon their fun.

The afternoon proved rather warm for exercise, even the gentle one of croquet. After finishing a long game, the whole party felt ready to agree to Ella's proposal of a rest and a cool drink. So, Mr. Ward was free to attend to Lily when she came rushing up to him. The rest of the children followed more slowly.

"Papa," she said, throwing herself across his knee as he sat upon the grass. "Daisy said we oughtn't to say 'upon our words and honors!' Oughtn't we? Will you teach us about taking God's name in vain now? It's the most important part of our party, but I forgot all about the swearing class until Daisy said that."

"Indeed," said Mr. Ward, lifting Lily to a seat upon his knee and smiling. The other girls laughed at her speech. "I am quite willing to have a little talk with you all on this subject. First, tell me what you want to know."

"Daisy is so awfully particular, Mr. Ward," said Minnie, in a hurt tone. "She won't let us say anything. At least, she says everything is wrong."

"Everything?" said Mr. Ward. "That is bad. Does Daisy want you all to keep silence? That must spoil your play."

"Oh, no!" said Minnie, "not that. She says such lots of things are wrong to say. Why Sir, she won't say 'upon her word and honor,' because she doesn't think it is right."

"Why do you want her to say it?" asked Mr. Ward.

"I was just going to tell them all a secret. I wanted her to promise on her sacred word and honor she would never tell. She wouldn't do it."

"So Daisy is apt to break her promises, is she?" said the gentleman. He smiled at Daisy, which told very plainly that he was only joking.

"Oh, no Sir," said Minnie. "Daisy always tells the truth and never does what she says she won't. At least, we never knew her to do it; did we, girls?"

A chorus of young voices raised in Daisy's favor.

"And yet you cannot trust her unless she swears to what she promises," said Mr. Ward.

"Swears, Sir!" said Minnie. "I'm sure I don't want her to swear. Word and honor are not bad words, are they?"

"Not in themselves, certainly," answered Mr. Ward. "Many a thing becomes bad and hurtful if put to a wrong purpose. Now to swear is to say, by some word or person which you consider holy and sacred, that you will or will not do, that you have or have not done, a certain thing. Suppose some man stood accused of a crime. A judge was about to try him and punish him if he found him guilty. The court thought that I knew whether or not the man had done the crime. So I am called to the court. In court, I promise that I will tell the truth, the whole truth, and nothing but the truth. To make sure of this I lay my hand on the Bible, God's holy Word, and call upon Him to hear me tell what I know. This is considered a very solemn thing, even by many who have little care or respect for God in other ways. It is called swearing or taking the oath."

"Shame on them," said Lily, indignantly. "They ought to know you would never tell a story, Papa. And to go and make you swear, too! I wouldn't do it if I were you. I'd tell them the third commandment and run away fast from them."

"If this is done in the fear of God and as a prayer that He will hear and help us tell the truth, then it is not taking His name in vain, Lily," said Mr. Ward. "To take the oath and not tell the truth is considered, even by men, a crime, a crime called perjury. If found guilty of this crime, the law severely punishes a person. When the life of another depends on the truth being told, taking an oath becomes wise and perhaps necessary. However, it can hardly be necessary for one little girl at play with another to have to swear by a promise. For to say, 'by your sacred word and honor,' becomes a sort of swearing, or oath taking, that what you say is true."

"Then we'll make a rule not to say it anymore," said Lily. "We didn't know it was naughty before, Papa. Please tell us now about other words. Daisy says we must not say 'mercy,' and 'gracious,' and 'heavens,' and maybe we must not; but why is that swearing? Swearing is taking God's name in vain. How do such words take His name in vain if we don't speak it? She thinks playing with the Bible or saying its words when playing is taking God's name in vain, too. Is it?"

"I will tell you," said Mr. Ward. "Suppose, Lily, some king or queen or the president of our own country came here. Would you not wish to behave with politeness and respect in your manner and speech?"

"Um-m-m, I don't know," answered Lily, doubtfully. "I guess I'd behave as saucy to them as to anyone else."

Mr. Ward saw this would not do, at least not for Lily. He must go higher than earthly rulers.

"Suppose then," he said, "that Jesus came down among us. We could see Him with our eyes, walking and talking with us. What would you all do?"

"I'd fall down and worship Him," said Minnie.

"I'd listen to every word He said. I would never speak one myself for fear I should miss one of His," said Daisy. "Then I'd remember them all the days of my life."

"Dear child," said Mr. Ward, laying his hand fondly on hers. "I believe you do treasure your Lord's words and try to live according to them."

"I'd ask Him to put His hand on my head and bless me. He blessed those other little children when He lived on earth before," said Lola softly.

"So would I. And I am glad no disciples would forbid us to come to Him," said Lily. "I suppose they thought Jesus would not care about children; but He did, didn't He?" The little child laid her hand lovingly against her father's cheek. "I'd keep very close to Him all the time He was here and take fast hold of His hand. I wouldn't be troublesome but just keep as still as a mouse. I'd give Him everything of mine that He wanted."

"So you would all show your love and reverence for Him," said Mr. Ward. "You would try not to sadden or offend Him by treating His name or His presence with the least carelessness. You would show Him that you honored His name and felt blessed by His presence; is it not so?"

"Yes Sir," came from the older as well as the younger children.

"Suppose after He left, He sent you each a letter. In the letter He told you what He wanted you to do and how to love and serve Him. The letter gave you all the advice, help, and comfort you would ever need. How would you treat that letter?"

"I'd keep it all my life and take such good care of it," said Rosie.

"I'd read it, and read it, and read it; and kiss it, and kiss it, and kiss it," said Lily. "Then I'd care for it so carefully!"

"And so would I, and I, and I," said the rest, satisfied to have Lily speak for them.

"And if you saw anyone misusing that letter, how would you feel?" asked Mr. Ward.

"I'd feel very upset with them," answered Lily. "I think I wouldn't love them anymore, except if it was you, Papa, or Mama or Elly or anyone of my own that I have to love. Then I'd cry and ask you not to treat my Jesus' letter so."

"You mean the Bible is Jesus' letter to us, don't you, Sir?" asked Daisy.

"Yes, I do. Children, our Lord's presence is here among us as much as when He lived as man on earth. His ear hears our words of love and praise or those of carelessness and disrespect. His eye sees the use we make of the precious Word He has given us. We forget this when we use His book carelessly or when we take His name lightly without thought. When we do that we take His name in vain and that displeases Him."

"But, Mr. Ward," said Minnie, "it is not cursing and swearing to say 'mercy,' 'gracious,' and 'good Lord,' is it?"

"Not cursing?" asked Mr. Ward. "Certainly! Cursing uses God's name profanely or to call on Him to destroy us or other people. This is a most terrible sin. Satan wants us to use words like 'golly' or 'gosh' for 'God,' 'darn' for 'damn,' 'gee' for 'Jesus,' and 'heck' for 'hell.' These words are often used as Satan's substitutes in our conversations or to call on God to destroy us or other people.

"However, Minnie, the use of such words in play or thoughtlessness is not only cursing but a bad habit. It leads to worse. Suppose a man breaks open a bank and takes all the money from it. Is that stealing?"

"Why, yes Sir," answered Minnie.

"And suppose you take candy belonging to your sister. That is a small thing compared to robbing a bank. However, is it not stealing all the same?"

"Yes Sir, if I behaved so bad as to take Julia's candy, I'm afraid I'd steal something worse sometime."

"Now," said the gentleman, "you see why it is unwise to use such expressions. It is, as Lily says, a kind of little swearing, but it leads to worse. Besides it is very useless. You can surely believe one another without saying 'upon your sacred word and honor,' 'as sure as you live,' 'heaven knows,' and so forth. You gain nothing by this sin, even of this world's good; no pleasure, nor profit. It is only an idle, useless habit that displeases the holy ear of our Lord. Goodness, mercy and graciousness belong to the Almighty. Jesus warns us in Matthew 5:33-37, 'Thou shalt not forswear thyself, but shalt perform unto the Lord thine oaths. But I say unto you, swear not at all; neither by heaven; for it is God's throne. Nor by the earth; for it is his footstool; neither by Jerusalem; for it is the city of the great King. Neither shalt thou swear by thy head, because thou canst not make one hair white or black. But let your communication be, Yea, yea; Nay, nay; for what-soever is more than these cometh of evil.'

"We must take heed that we do not speak of what belongs to Him in a careless way. And now I believe we have had enough talk on this subject for this afternoon. You did not ask your friends here so I might lecture them."

"Oh yes, I did, Papa!" said Lily. "We all deserved it very much, especially the big girls. Papa, do you believe the Lord troubles Himself to know where the girls put an old, worn-out cushion and such things? If He does, ought we to say He does?"

"God knows everything, Lily. He knows even the smallest trifle event, but it is very wrong to say in a careless way, 'the Lord knows.' The very thought that His eyes and His ears always notice every word, look, and our feelings should make all of us more careful how we use His holy name. I am glad this question came up among you. Carelessness in using God's name and other sacred words and in quoting Scripture... talking Bible, my Lily calls it... has become too common a habit. We older ones, as well as the young people in Glenwood, too often fall into the custom. Many of us have the constant need of the prayer, 'Set a watch, O Lord, upon my mouth; keep the door of my lips.'"

"Daisy brought the matter to our attention," said honest Cora. "I, for one, have offended God in this way and have set a bad example to the rest. I believe the little ones have learned it from us older girls. We should thank Daisy for teaching us a better lesson."

Chapter 8

DAISY'S NAME

"Indeed, haven't my words come true, Sir? Didn't I tell you she was a little lady?" said Betty MaCarthy. She stood with her hands on her hips, her head on one side, and her honest face one broad glow of delight and satisfaction. She gazed at the dainty-looking, yet humble, little creature who stood before her, her young face bright with as much pleasure as Betty's own.

Daisy's old friend had come to live at Mrs. Forster's. The lady had wanted a laundrywoman. Because Betty had once held that job in her father's family, she thought she might know of one. She asked the General to inquire.

When he asked, Betty eagerly answered she would like the job herself. She had become tired of her present position. She knew of another woman who wanted to purchase her stall. For her heart felt sore for the child, Betty said. To live where she could see Daisy everyday and to work once more with "Miss Gertrude" would make her very happy. Then she would try to put Jack out with some gardener to learn his trade.

The General talked the matter over with his wife. They remembered the kind and generous care shown to their Daisy by these poor people. They not only told Betty she could come live with them, but they also put Jack to work under their gardener. Although, they really had no need for any more hands about the place. Thus did the kindness of this Irishwoman come back to her and bless her.

Daisy knew nothing of this arrangement. One afternoon Mrs. Forster said to her, "I am going to speak to the new laundrywoman and gardener's boy. Come with me, Daisy." Half wondering, the little girl obeyed.

Her surprise soon changed into delight and gratitude when she saw who the new workers were. In spite of all the pleasure she felt in her new way of life, Daisy's loving heart often longed for the old friends. They had helped her in her time of need. She wanted not only to see them, but to share some of her many comforts with them. How happy Daisy felt when her eye fell upon the two figures standing by the back door. She knew that they had come to live in the same place with her.

Daisy flew at Betty, throwing both arms about her neck. She covered her broad, smiling face with warm kisses. Betty returned them, holding her fast in both arms. Then standing back and looking at her from head to foot, Betty spoke to the General the words of approval you read at the beginning of this chapter.

"And isn't she fit for a princess?" she continued, unable to keep back her pleasure at the child's improved appearance. "Isn't she fit for a princess? Saacyfuts or no Saacyfuts, her folks would have a right to the name if they found her now. Sure, I'd be saacy myself to have a child like that. And her not a bit spoiled, but just as loving and free-like as when she had no one but me and Jack."

The Forsters told Daisy she could show Betty and Jack the neat little wash house. The house, shadowed by a fine clump of trees, had the laundry on the first floor and two small bedrooms upstairs. Betty expressed over and over again her satisfaction at the change in her life. Far better, she thought, to stand at the wash-tub or ironing table breathing the sweet country air, than to do the same at her stall in the hot, dusty, crowded city.

As for Jack, when he saw the splendid garden and knew he would work among those lovely flowers, he could not contain himself. He shouted and shouted and turned somersault after somersault. Finally Betty reminded him that Margaret or "Miss Daisy" was a lady now and he should mind his manners before her.

However, Daisy acted like her old self, free from any pride in her new position. Jack found it hard not to still think of her as the little orphan he had pitied and loved for so long. His manners came to his mind with much more force by the sight of the gray-haired old Scot gardener. His playfulness ceased at once in the presence of the man he would work under.

Meanwhile, General and Mrs. Forster talked on a very interesting subject. Betty's words about Daisy's lost family gave the lady a new idea.

"Frank," she said to her husband, "did you notice what Betty said about Daisy's family?"

"Yes," he answered. "I hope she won't turn Daisy's head and make her vain with her praise and flattery."

"I'm not worried," said his wife. "Daisy has a right to her name, the modest, unaffected little girl. She has too much sense to become spoiled by the overflowing of Betty's affection. Don't you know that the Irish often say saacy when they mean proud?"

"Oh, yes. I have often noticed it in people of Betty's class," answered the General. "What has that to do with Daisy's family?"

"Is it not possible that their name is Proudfoot or Proudfit, instead of the "Saacyfut" Betty says?"

The General laughed heartily. "Hardly, I think," he said, "and yet... I do not know. It may be."

"We will ask Daisy when she comes," said Mrs. Forster. "If Proudfoot was their name, she might remember it when she hears the name spoken. She can hardly have forgotten it so entirely that she would not recognize it. If we know her name, that will help locate her family." Mrs. Forster spoke the last words more slowly.

"Yes," said her husband. Then he gave words to the thought which made her half unwilling to utter them, "And if found, we must give up our Daisy."

"But we must search for them," she said. "If we don't, I shall feel as if we had found a lovely jewel that we tried to hide from the rightful owner. I know what terrible longings must fill her mother's heart." A tear dropped from Mrs. Forster's eye on her baby's face, as she clasped it more tenderly than ever in her arms.

"Daisy," said the General that evening, "did you ever hear the name of Proudfoot?"

Daisy started, drew a quick, gasping breath and suddenly threw herself into his arms. "That is it!" she cried, in a rapid, excited manner. "That is it! That is my name; that is what they called Papa and Mama! I never heard it since; but I know it now. I am Daisy Proudfoot, I am, I am!"

The excited child remembered nothing further as she calmed down. The recollection of her name, Proudfoot, filled her with happiness. Still, she could not tell where she belonged.

Betty, too, when asked if Proudfoot was the name of Daisy's mother answered, "Sure, it was Ma'am. Didn't I say so all along? Only she always denied it."

The matter of the name settled, General Forster again placed advertisements in the papers. This time he said if any family, named Proudfoot, had lost a child at sea, they might hear of her at such and such a place. He felt sad to think he might have to part with Daisy, but also felt he must try again to trace her family.

Daisy knew nothing of the new search. She felt content and happy in her home and among her new friends. They thought it best not to give her fresh hopes of finding family who might never come.

Although still known as Daisy Forster by all in Glenwood, Daisy and the Forsters felt a satisfaction in knowing her true name.

Days, weeks, and months went by. Still no one came to seek the Daisy blossom which had been transplanted to such pleasant soil. And there it grew and flourished and did its Master's work, proving how much even a simple floweret can do by its own example, teaching others to honor Him.

Her schoolmates thought a lot of her opinion and profited by the simple lesson she had taught them. They tried to break themselves of the foolish and sinful habit of using sacred names and things in a careless and unthinking manner.

Not only the little girls, but the older ones and even Miss Collins, learned from our Daisy. They tried to remember the ever present Lord's ear. They now knew that thoughtless words which dishonored Him or His belongings displeased Him.

Perhaps they gave more heed to Daisy's words than they would have done to any of the other girls. Because such a half-mystery surrounded her, the others treated Daisy with tenderness. They checked their careless speech for her sake at first.

As they learned to think more about it, they talked with care for a better and higher reason. Until, at last, they rid themselves of the bad habit. If, by chance, a careless word came from the lips of any child, the surprised and reproving looks of her companions told her of her wrong and punished her sufficiently.

The good influence spread far and wide. Since the little ones behaved so carefully, their parents and older friends felt that they must also. So it came to pass that the families of Glenwood held God's name and Word in true reverence and honor.

Nearly a year passed by bringing the Daisy and her sister-flowerets to another spring.

Chapter 9

THE LOST FOUND

"Is that you, Daisy?"

"Yes, Sir. Is that you, Uncle Frank?" answered Daisy, playfully.

"Well, I thought it was this morning when I went to town, but I am doubtful of it now."

"Why?" asked Daisy, laughing as she reached up on tiptoe to offer a welcome home kiss to her uncle.

"Baby Daisy has no doubts, at least," said Mrs. Forster. She placed her little daughter, all coos and smiles, in her father's arms. "Let her pull your hair a little to convince you of the fact."

"I will still find it difficult to believe," said the General. "Today a man sat in the railway car that looked so like me, in face, height, and figure, that some of my friends mistook him for me. Others accused me of having a brother whom I have never claimed. He sat two or three seats in front of me and I could not help being amused. Ward came in, nodded to my double saying, "How are you, General?" He passed on to me, where he stopped and looked from one to the other with a mixture of surprised curiosity that was amusing. Then he and many others asked for information which I could not give. I hope the stranger will keep himself out of mischief while he is in Glenwood. If not, I may be held responsible for his wrong doings."

"Did he come to Glenwood?" asked Daisy.

"Yes, he did. I left him standing on the platform at the station. I hardly knew whether my own carriage belonged to him or to me. However, he made no claim as I stepped into it."

"Who was he?" asked Mrs. Forster. "Did you not find out?"

"No, no one could tell me. I could not go and ask the man who he was just because he resembled me so much. There, there, little woman," as the baby gave a vigorous pull at his hair. "I've had enough of Mama's proof. I am satisfied that no other man than Frank submit to such usage at these tiny hands. I believe this stranger came up to look at Beechgrove, which is for rent. I heard him asking the railway porter for directions."

Two weeks passed by, no one saw the stranger who looked so like General Forster again. In fact, after that evening the General and his wife did not even think of him.

This was not so for Daisy. She thought often of him with a half wish that she might see him; why, she scarcely knew herself. She never spoke of it. Daisy, a shy, quiet child, kept her ideas and wishes pretty much to herself, unless someone whom she loved or trusted drew them out. Neither the General nor Mrs. Forster suspected what was working in her mind.

They regarded her idea that the General looked so like her own papa as a childish fancy. They thought she saw a likeness between the two only because she loved and admired them both. Never would they have imagined the dreams and wondering that the child did over this unseen stranger, a stranger who had had such a passing interest for them.

Meanwhile, it became certain that Beechgrove would no longer remain empty. The agency removed the signs advertising it for rent and the house went through a thorough cleaning.

The General and his wife never gossiped or concerned themselves about their neighbor's affairs. They did not trouble themselves about the matter. The curious who asked questions received no satisfaction from old Dr. Harding, who had charge of the property.

All Miss Collins' young scholars, however, felt concerned about Beechgrove and with good reason. A large birdcage belonged to the place, containing many rare and beautiful birds. The former owner, who was fond of children, often invited the young people of Glenwood to see these birds. Since Dr. Harding began caring for the place, no child had seen the birdcage. Our young friends hoped the new occupants at Beechgrove would once again allow them to visit.

One morning when Daisy came to school, she found the rest of the class grouped about Mattie

Prime and Rosie Pierson. They passed Beechgrove on their way to Miss Collins'.

"The new people have moved into Beechgrove," said Violet Swan, when Daisy asked what they were talking about. "Mattie and Rosie saw a little girl there this morning. We feel happy about a little girl living there. Perhaps her papa will let other children see the birds."

"She's a very little thing," said Rosie, "She can't speak plain."

"But she's very cute," said Mattie. "As we passed by the gate, she called out to us, 'Itty dirls, itty dirls.' When we stopped she put her face through the rails to kiss us and handed us some flowers she had."

"What is her name?" asked Daisy.

"We asked her, but could not make out what she said. Mamy Modwit, it sounded like; but she did speak so crooked," said Mattie.

"Do you know," said Rosie, "she looked like Daisy. Don't you think, Mattie?"

"Why, so she does," said Mattie. "Isn't that funny? Only Daisy's eyes always look sorry except when she laughs or speaks. That little girl's eyes danced with mischief and laughter."

"How big was she?" asked Lola.

"Oh, about as large as your sister Bertie, not near old enough to come to school."

"I suppose they have no other children but her," said Fanny Delisle. "Willie saw the family come yesterday. He said he saw only the lady, the gentleman, the little girl, and servants. Maybe they won't think about letting us see the birdcage again if they don't have older children."

This short conversation put an end to the half hope, half wish, Daisy had held in her heart. Even if the stranger who looked so like General Forster had rented Beechgrove, he could not belong to her. The description of this family did not match her own. She had Papa, Mama, little brother Theodore, and a baby sister, a very little baby. Only, this child of three years old or more seemed to belong to the newcomers. She had no sister so old.

Daisy reasoned this all out for herself with a sad, disappointed little heart. She forgot that time had not stood still with her own family any more than it had with her. Changes might have come to them as well as to her.

This talk took place on Friday. Daisy and her playmates neither saw nor heard anything more of the strangers until Sunday came. Then a strange and happy thing came to pass and in such a wonderful way. "Just like a book thing," Lily Ward afterwards said.

It was the loveliest of Sabbath days and everything seemed to feel it.

"What day is it, Bertie?" asked Mr. Swan as his youngest daughter stood on the porch steps ready for church.

"Jesus' happy Sunday," answered the little one. "Oh, didn't He make a nice one!"

People other than Bertie thought it a nice May Sunday, too. A busy little breeze carried with it the perfume of the apple-blossoms. The sweet aroma passed through the open windows of the church. It wandered around among the aisles, pillars, and pews. Sometimes it fluttered the leaves of a book or fanned some cheek flushed from a walk in the almost summer heat. A robin swung himself lightly to and fro on the branch of one of the old elms outside the church door. The bird poured forth his hymn of praise, while from afar came the answering notes of his mates. The voices of the children in Sunday school mingled with his song as they sang the closing hymn.

Then they came trooping in gently and with soft footsteps, as became the house of God. Learning to honor His name and His word had also taught them to honor the place where He was worshipped. They took their places beside their parents and friends.

Watching them from one of the pews which ran by the side of the pulpit, were a pair of roguish, dancing eyes. Rosie Pierson and Mattie Prime recognized them at once. They belonged to the little girl who had peeped at them through the railing of the Beechgrove grounds. Now her eyes peeped over the top of the pew, as she stood at its foot, her hands crossed upon it and her chin resting upon them. What a bright, merry, laughing face she had and how like Daisy's! General and Mrs. Forster noticed it from their seat.

Beside the little girl sat a gentleman, half turned from the congregation, his face partly shaded by his hand. However, there was no doubt that he was the man who looked so like the General. Mrs. Forster saw the likeness at once, even in the turn and shape of his head. Beyond him a lady sat in deep mourning, closely veiled.

"Frank must find out who they are," said Mrs. Forster to herself. "That child is so like Daisy. Can it be... oh, can it be?" Then she tried to collect her thoughts and bring them back to the service of Him whom she had come to worship.

Daisy came in a little behind the rest of her class. She had lingered for a word with her teacher. She took her seat. Almost immediately her eye fell on the newcomers to Glenwood. Mrs. Forster saw her start to flush all over her neck and face. She pressed her small hands tightly together as if trying to keep back some exclamation which rose to her lips. With a beating heart the child watched the strangers, striving in vain to get a better view of the face of the gentleman. Her gaze went from him to the veiled lady and then to the little girl.

The bell ceased tolling, the congregation had gathered, the hour of service had come. The clergyman rose in the pulpit.

At that moment the lady drew aside her veil. Before Dr. Parker opened his lips, a little voice rang through the still church.

"Mama! Oh, my own mama!"

What a tale those few words told. What a world of longing, of love, of joy they held.

The stranger lady... ah! no stranger to our Daisy... started to her feet and stretched out her hands. With a little cry she sank fainting into the arms of the gentleman who had also suddenly arisen.

They carried her out. General and Mrs. Forster followed with the excited, trembling Daisy. And so, the father and mother found the long-lost child.

Who could describe it? Who could find words for the joy, the wonder, the gratitude of those concerned? Who could tell the sympathy which filled the hearts of all in that congregation? Tears dimmed their eyes. Their hearts filled with adoration as the minister called on all to give thanks. They thanked the Lord for the great mercy shown to those long-parted parents and their little one!

Now there is a little more to tell. Daisy's mama and the little sister whom she remembered as a tiny baby had been rescued from the sinking ship with some of the other passengers. Unable to trace their lost treasure and believing that the boat containing her had sunk, the parents had gone overseas. There they remained until a few months before this time. They had never seen the advertisements which might have told them she was still living.

Daisy told her story. Betty helped out where the little girl's memory failed. Some of the past was a blank because of that long illness. Betty laughed and cried by turns and would hear of no praise or thanks for what she had done. She declared that Miss Daisy had done her and Jack far more good than she received. She taught them to mind their tongues before God Almighty.

Although General and Mrs. Forster had to give up their darling Daisy, they did not have to part with her altogether. She lived so near them that they saw her everyday. Indeed, the two families became almost as one and Daisy felt as if she had two homes.

The little brother, whom Daisy remembered so well, had died only a few weeks before her father and mother came to Glenwood.

So the Daisy blossom, once parted from its parent stem and cast by the wayside where stranger hands had gathered and lovingly tended it, once again became planted in the soil where it belonged. The Daisy blossom had done the Master's work and scattered the good seed which budded for His glory. Thus proving well, that those who honor the Lord, He will delight to honor.